W9-ARA-195

J BIO ALI
Burgan, Michael.
Muhammad Ali : American
champion /

GRAPHIC BIOGRAPHIES

MUHAMMAD ALI

AMERICAN CHAMPION

by Michael Burgan

illustrated by Brian Bascle

Consultant:
Gerald Lyn Early
Professor of African and African American Studies
Washington University, St. Louis
editor, *The Muhammad Ali Reader*

Capstone
press®

Mankato, Minnesota

Graphic Library is published by Capstone Press,
151 Good Counsel Drive, P.O. Box 669, Mankato, Minnesota 56002.
www.capstonepress.com

1 2 3 4 5 6 12 11 10 09 08 07

Library of Congress Cataloging-in-Publication Data
Burgan, Michael.
 Muhammad Ali: American champion / by Michael Burgan; illustrated by Brian Bascle.
 p. cm. —(Graphic library. Graphic biographies)
 Summary: "In graphic novel format, tells the life story of dynamic heavyweight boxing champion
Muhammad Ali, who gained fame for his boxing skills, political views, and humanitarian efforts"—
Provided by publisher.
 Includes bibliographical references and index.
 ISBN-13: 978-1-4296-0153-5 (hardcover)
 ISBN-10: 1-4296-0153-1 (hardcover)
 1. Ali, Muhammad, 1942—Juvenile literature. 2. Boxers (Sports)—United States—Biography—
Juvenile literature. I. Bascle, Brian, ill. II. Title. III. Series.
GV1132.A4B87 2008
796.83092—dc22
[B]   2006103432

Designer	*Editor*
Bob Lentz	Christine Peterson

Editor's note: Direct quotations from primary sources are indicated by a yellow background.

Direct quotations appear on the following pages:
Page 5, quote by Joe Martin; page 7, 1960 poem by Muhammad Ali; page 8 (bottom), February 25,
 1964, quote by Ali; page 9, quote by Ali after his first victory over Liston; page 12, quote by Ali as
 recorded on February 17, 1966; page 16, quote by Ali on February 1, 1971; page 17, quote
 attributed to Ali during his March 1971 bout with Joe Frazier; page 19 (top), poem attributed to
 Ali; page 23 (top), quote by Ali prior to his 1980 fight with Larry Holmes; page 23 (bottom), quote
 attributed to Ali in the December 13, 1981, issue of the *New York Times*; all quotes as published in
 Muhammad Ali: His Life and Times by Thomas Hauser (New York: Simon and Schuster, 1991).
Page 8 (top), quote attributed to Ali, as published in *King of the World: Muhammad Ali and the Rise of
 an American Hero* by David Remnick (New York: Random House, 1998).
Page 14, quote attributed to Martin Luther King Jr., as published in *Muhammad Ali's Greatest Fight:
 Cassius Clay vs. The United States of America*, by Howard L. Bingham and Max Wallace
 (New York: M. Evans, 2000).
Page 19 (bottom), quote attributed to Ferdie Pacheco, as published in *Sound and Fury: Two Powerful
 Lives, One Fateful Friendship* by David Kindred (New York: Free Press, 2006).
Page 27 (top), from a letter written by Ali in 2000, as published in *Soul of a Butterfly:
 Reflections on Life's Journey* by Muhammad Ali (New York: Simon & Schuster, 2004).
Page 27 (bottom), quote attributed to Ali on the Muhammad Ali Institute web site
 (http://www.aliinstitute.louisville.edu).

MUHAMMAD ALI
AMERICAN CHAMPION

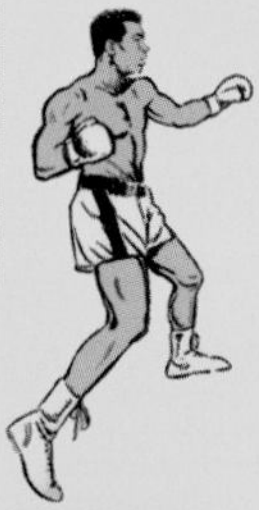

TABLE OF CONTENTS

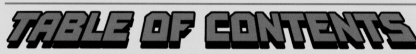

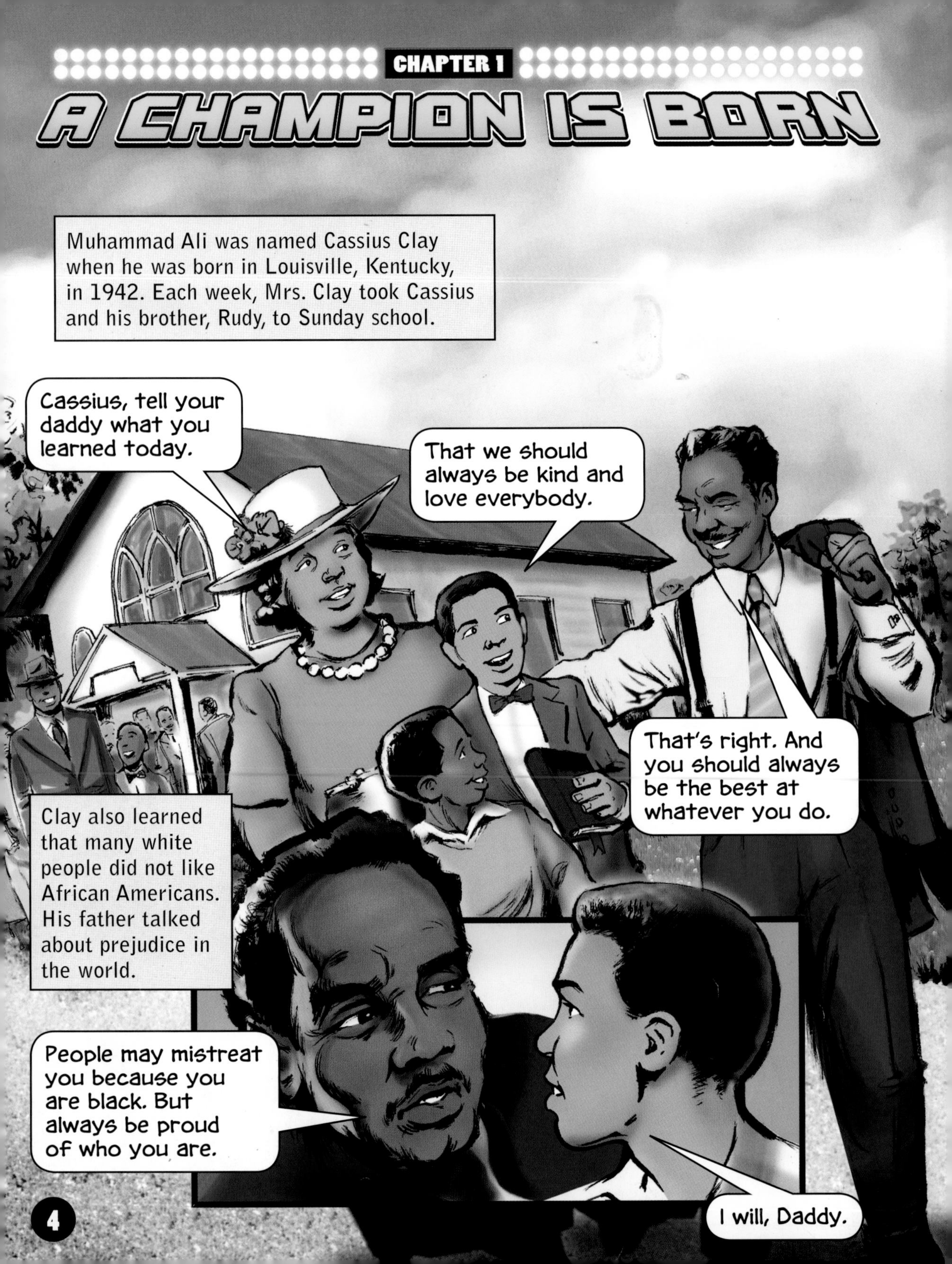
CHAPTER 1
A CHAMPION IS BORN
Muhammad Ali was named Cassius Clay when he was born in Louisville, Kentucky, in 1942. Each week, Mrs. Clay took Cassius and his brother, Rudy, to Sunday school.
Cassius, tell your daddy what you learned today.
That we should always be kind and love everybody.
That's right. And you should always be the best at whatever you do.
Clay also learned that many white people did not like African Americans. His father talked about prejudice in the world.
People may mistreat you because you are black. But always be proud of who you are.
I will, Daddy.

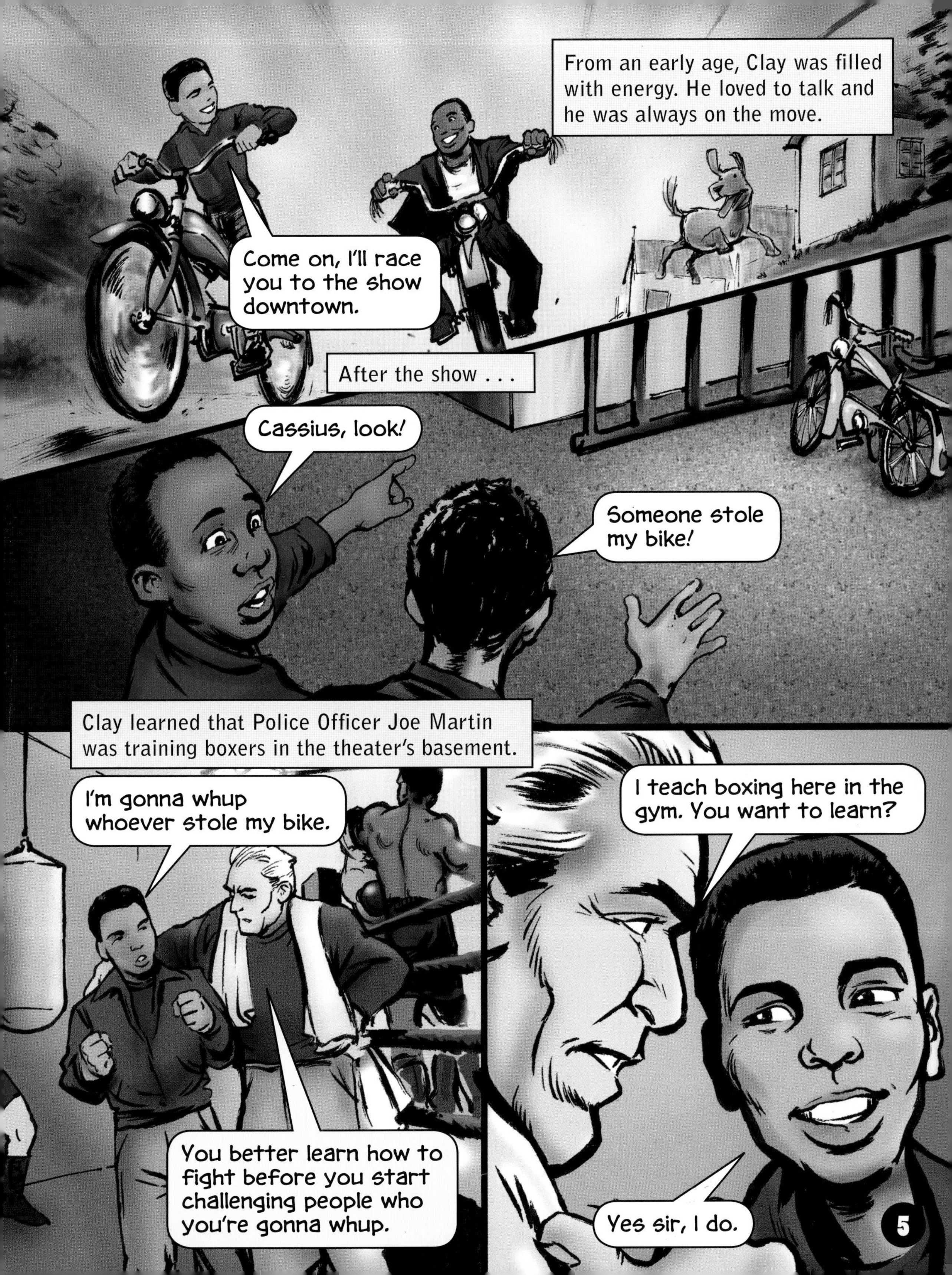
From an early age, Clay was filled with energy. He loved to talk and he was always on the move.
Come on, I'll race you to the show downtown.
After the show . . .
Cassius, look!
Someone stole my bike!
Clay learned that Police Officer Joe Martin was training boxers in the theater's basement.
I'm gonna whup whoever stole my bike.
You better learn how to fight before you start challenging people who you're gonna whup.
I teach boxing here in the gym. You want to learn?
Yes sir, I do.

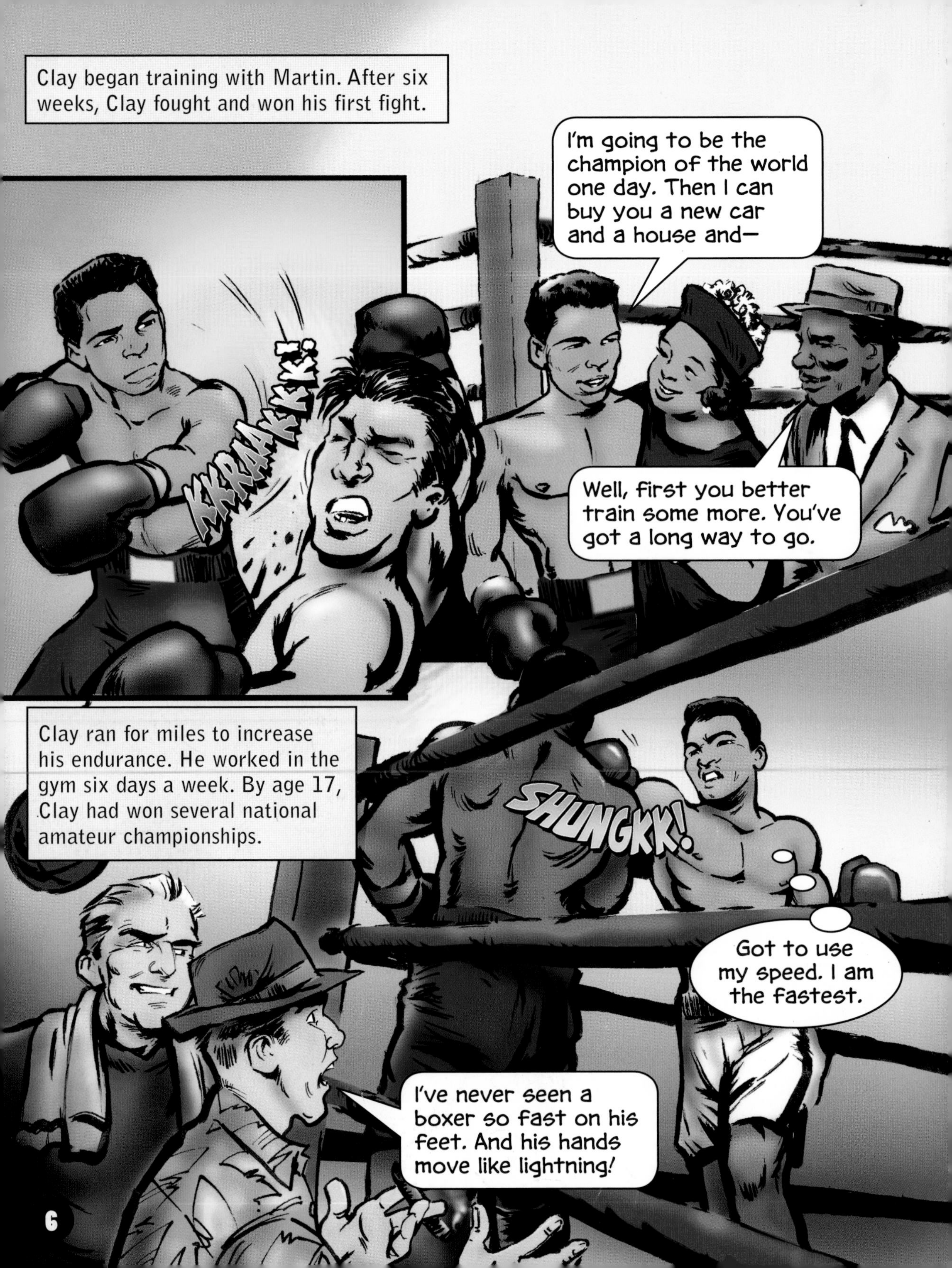
Clay began training with Martin. After six weeks, Clay fought and won his first fight.
KKRAAKKK!
I'm going to be the champion of the world one day. Then I can buy you a new car and a house and—
Well, first you better train some more. You've got a long way to go.
Clay ran for miles to increase his endurance. He worked in the gym six days a week. By age 17, Clay had won several national amateur championships.
SHUNGKK!
Got to use my speed. I am the fastest.
I've never seen a boxer so fast on his feet. And his hands move like lightning!

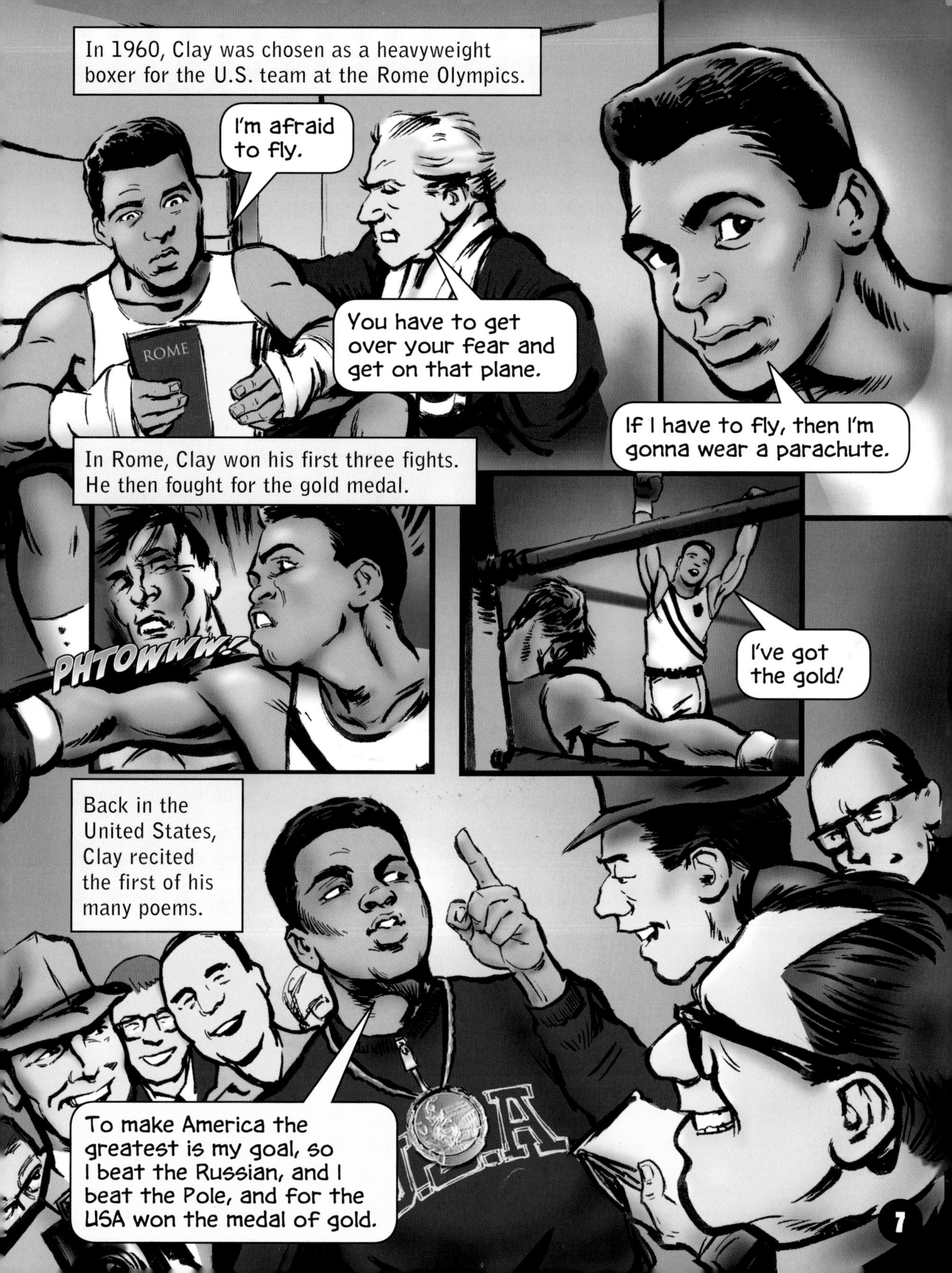
In 1960, Clay was chosen as a heavyweight boxer for the U.S. team at the Rome Olympics.
I'm afraid to fly.
ROME
You have to get over your fear and get on that plane.
If I have to fly, then I'm gonna wear a parachute.
In Rome, Clay won his first three fights. He then fought for the gold medal.
PHTOWWW!
I've got the gold!
Back in the United States, Clay recited the first of his many poems.
To make America the greatest is my goal, so I beat the Russian, and I beat the Pole, and for the USA won the medal of gold.

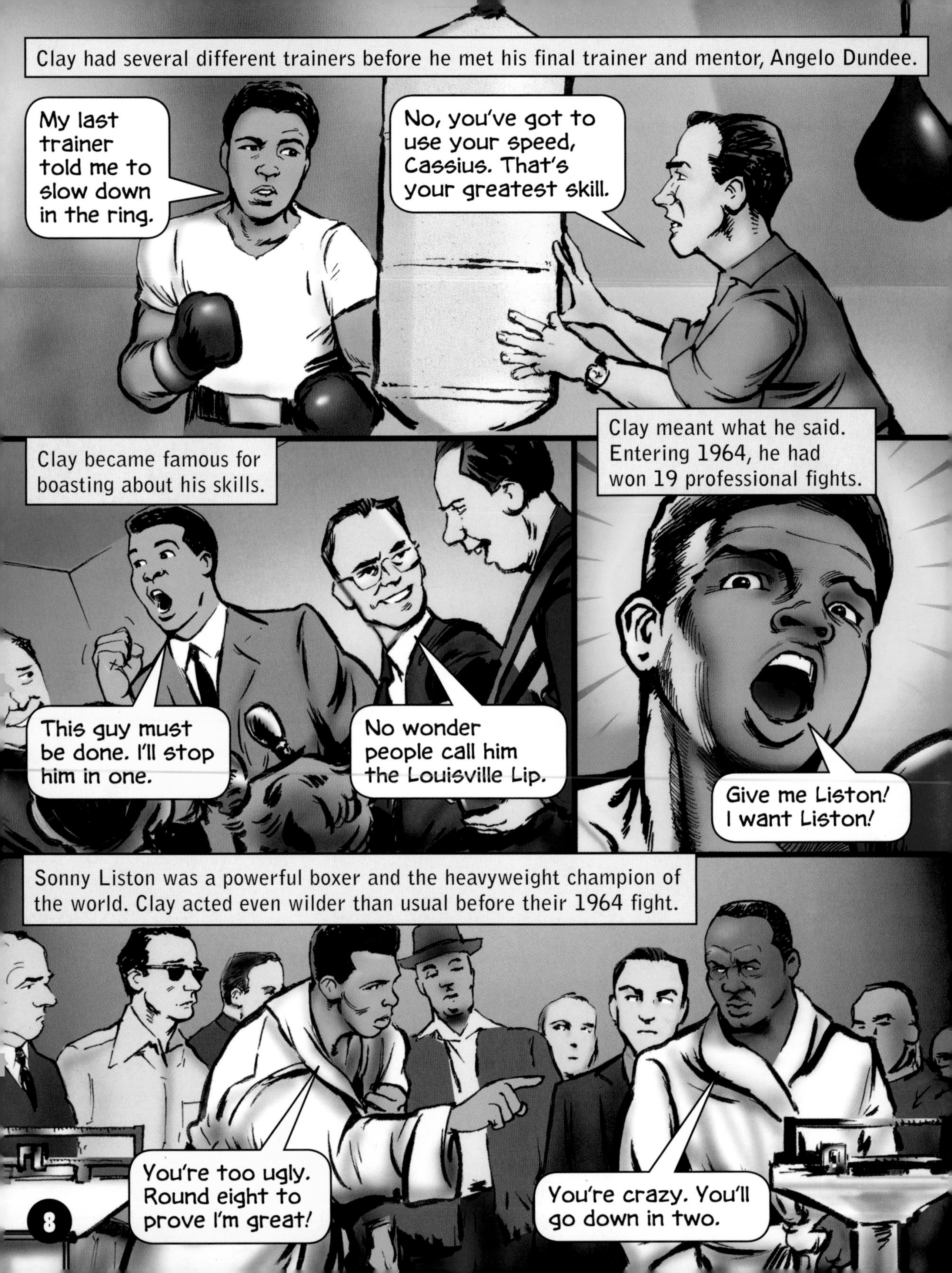

Clay had several different trainers before he met his final trainer and mentor, Angelo Dundee.
My last trainer told me to slow down in the ring.
No, you've got to use your speed, Cassius. That's your greatest skill.
Clay became famous for boasting about his skills.
This guy must be done. I'll stop him in one.
No wonder people call him the Louisville Lip.
Clay meant what he said. Entering 1964, he had won 19 professional fights.
Give me Liston! I want Liston!
Sonny Liston was a powerful boxer and the heavyweight champion of the world. Clay acted even wilder than usual before their 1964 fight.
You're too ugly. Round eight to prove I'm great!
You're crazy. You'll go down in two.

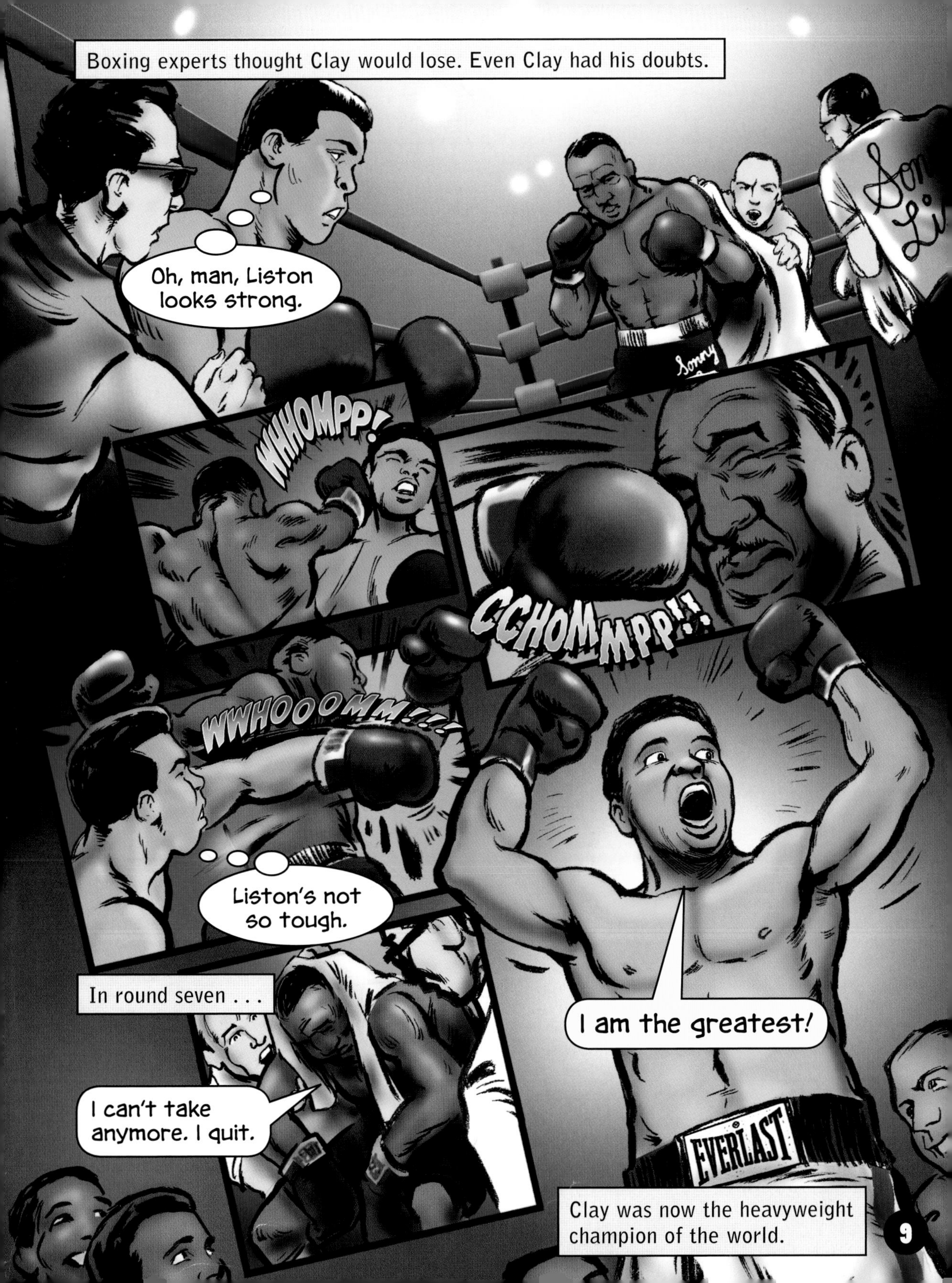
Boxing experts thought Clay would lose. Even Clay had his doubts.
Oh, man, Liston looks strong.
Sonny
WHHOMPP!
CCHOMMPP!!
WWHOOOMM!!!
Liston's not so tough.
In round seven . . .
I can't take anymore. I quit.
I am the greatest!
EVERLAST
Clay was now the heavyweight champion of the world.

CHAPTER 2
CHAMP NO MORE

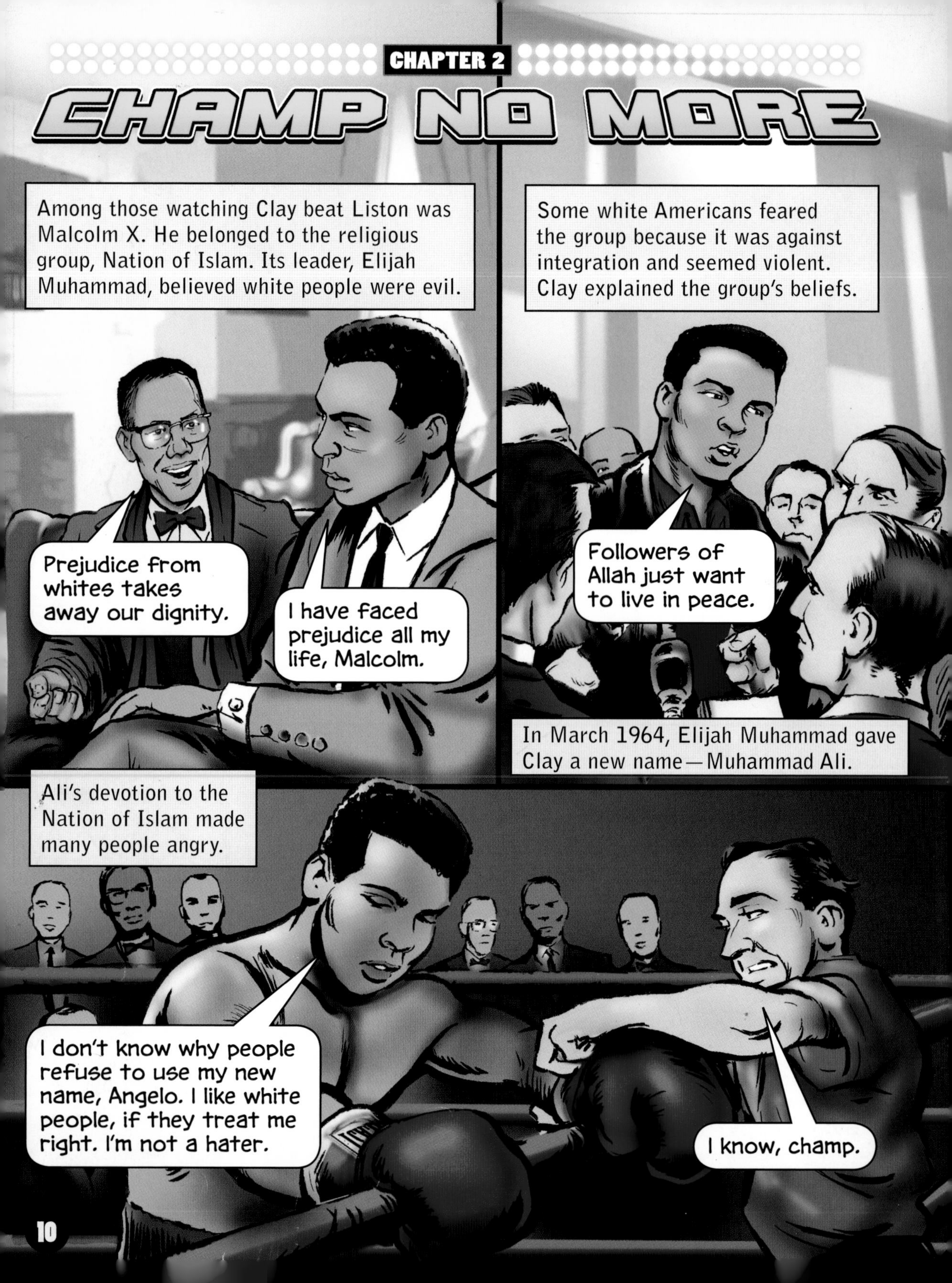

Among those watching Clay beat Liston was Malcolm X. He belonged to the religious group, Nation of Islam. Its leader, Elijah Muhammad, believed white people were evil.
Prejudice from whites takes away our dignity.
I have faced prejudice all my life, Malcolm.
Some white Americans feared the group because it was against integration and seemed violent. Clay explained the group's beliefs.
Followers of Allah just want to live in peace.
In March 1964, Elijah Muhammad gave Clay a new name—Muhammad Ali.
Ali's devotion to the Nation of Islam made many people angry.
I don't know why people refuse to use my new name, Angelo. I like white people, if they treat me right. I'm not a hater.
I know, champ.

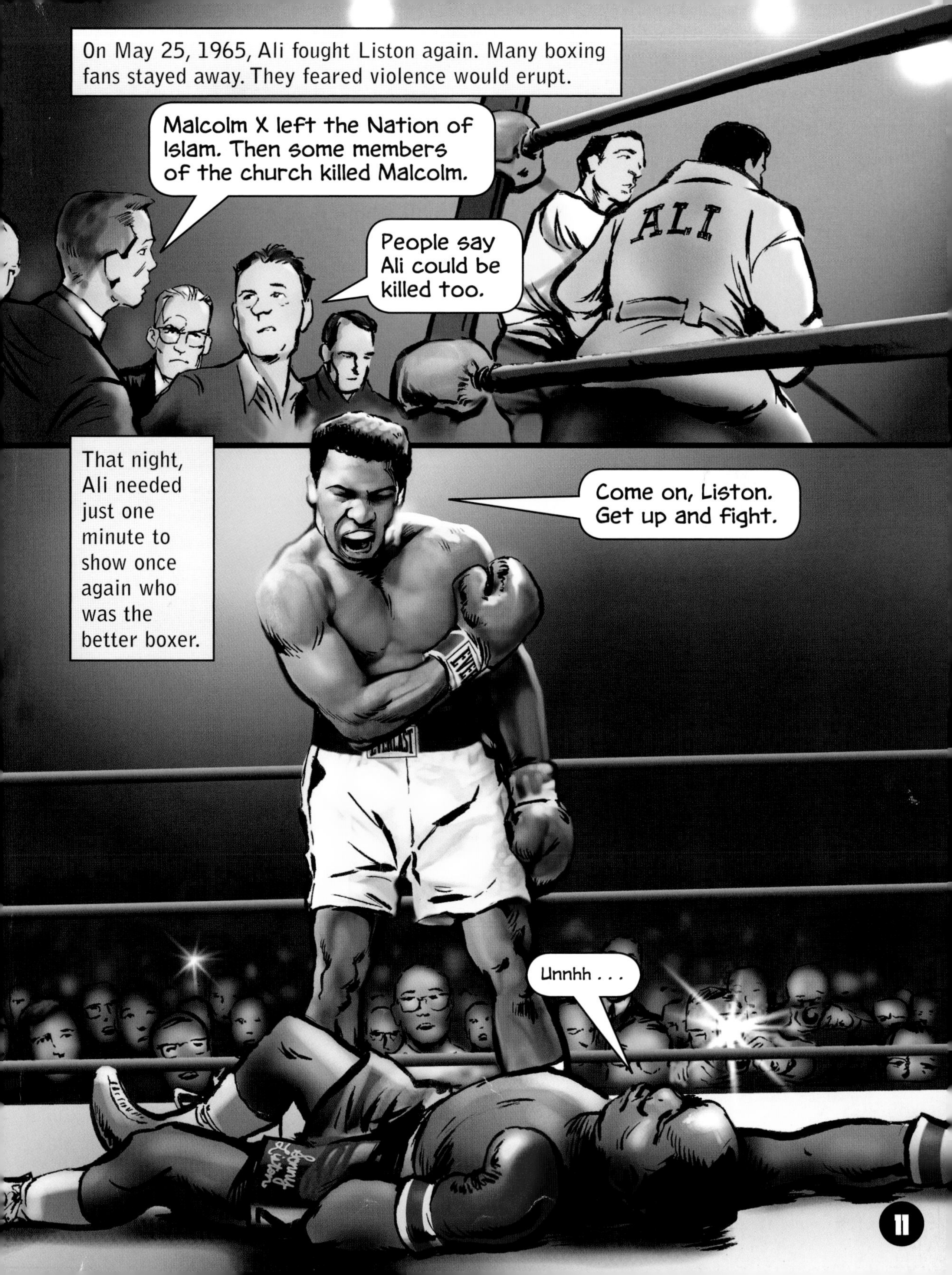
On May 25, 1965, Ali fought Liston again. Many boxing fans stayed away. They feared violence would erupt.
Malcolm X left the Nation of Islam. Then some members of the church killed Malcolm.
People say Ali could be killed too.
ALI
That night, Ali needed just one minute to show once again who was the better boxer.
Come on, Liston. Get up and fight.
EVERLAST
Unnhh . . .

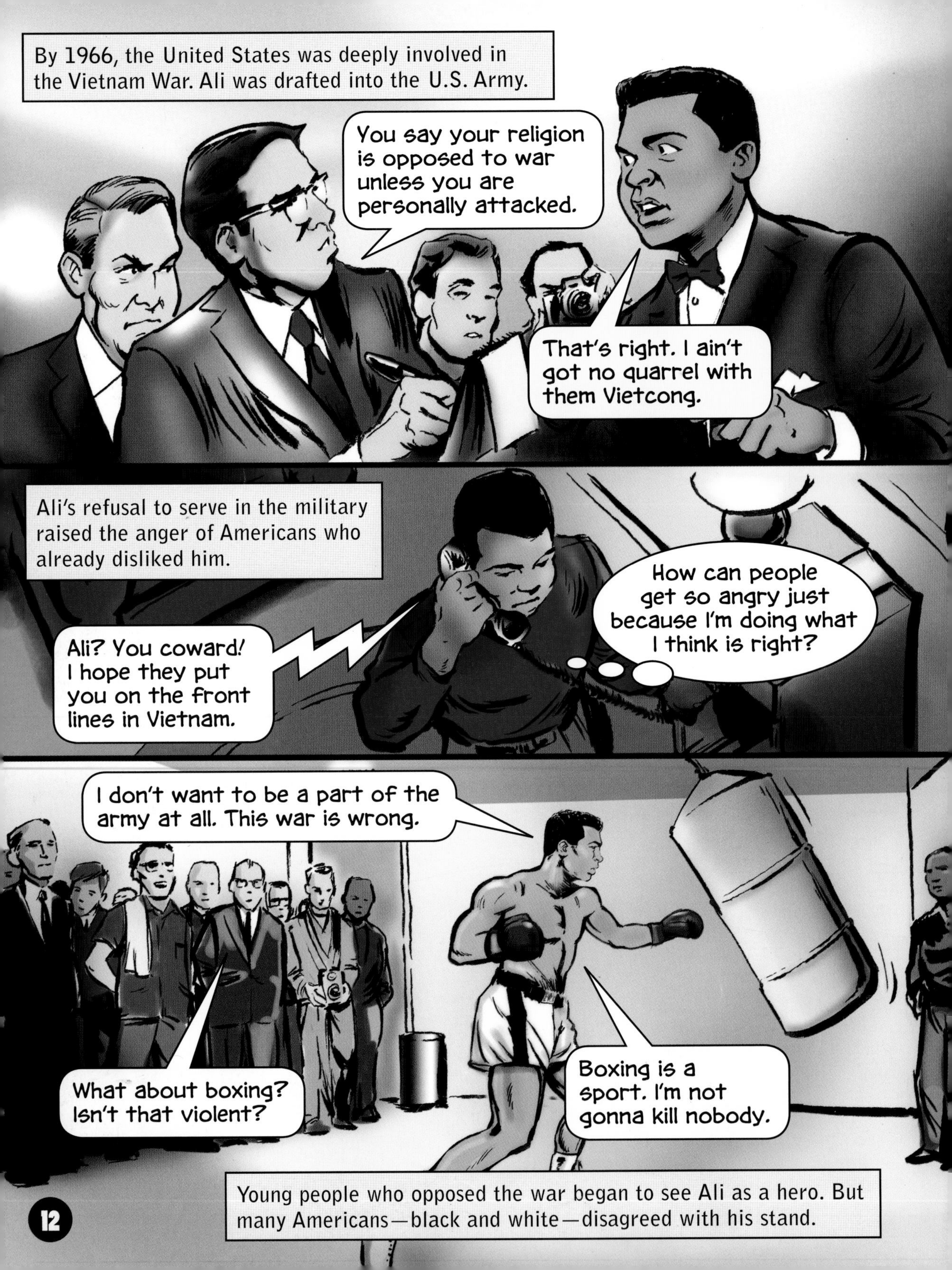
By 1966, the United States was deeply involved in the Vietnam War. Ali was drafted into the U.S. Army.
You say your religion is opposed to war unless you are personally attacked.
That's right. I ain't got no quarrel with them Vietcong.
Ali's refusal to serve in the military raised the anger of Americans who already disliked him.
Ali? You coward! I hope they put you on the front lines in Vietnam.
How can people get so angry just because I'm doing what I think is right?
I don't want to be a part of the army at all. This war is wrong.
What about boxing? Isn't that violent?
Boxing is a sport. I'm not gonna kill nobody.
Young people who opposed the war began to see Ali as a hero. But many Americans—black and white—disagreed with his stand.

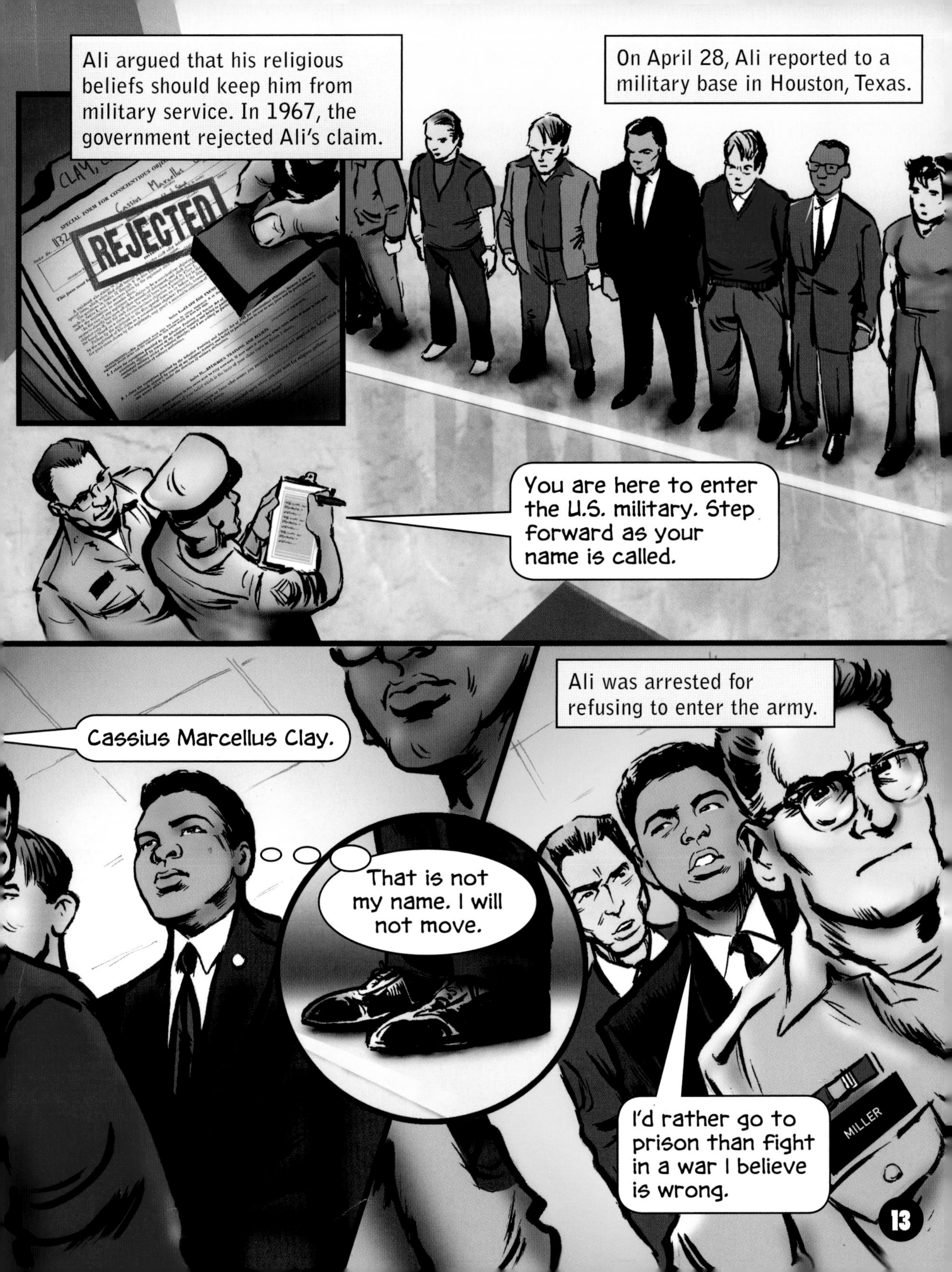

Ali argued that his religious beliefs should keep him from military service. In 1967, the government rejected Ali's claim.
REJECTED
On April 28, Ali reported to a military base in Houston, Texas.
You are here to enter the U.S. military. Step forward as your name is called.
Cassius Marcellus Clay.
That is not my name. I will not move.
Ali was arrested for refusing to enter the army.
I'd rather go to prison than fight in a war I believe is wrong.
MILLER

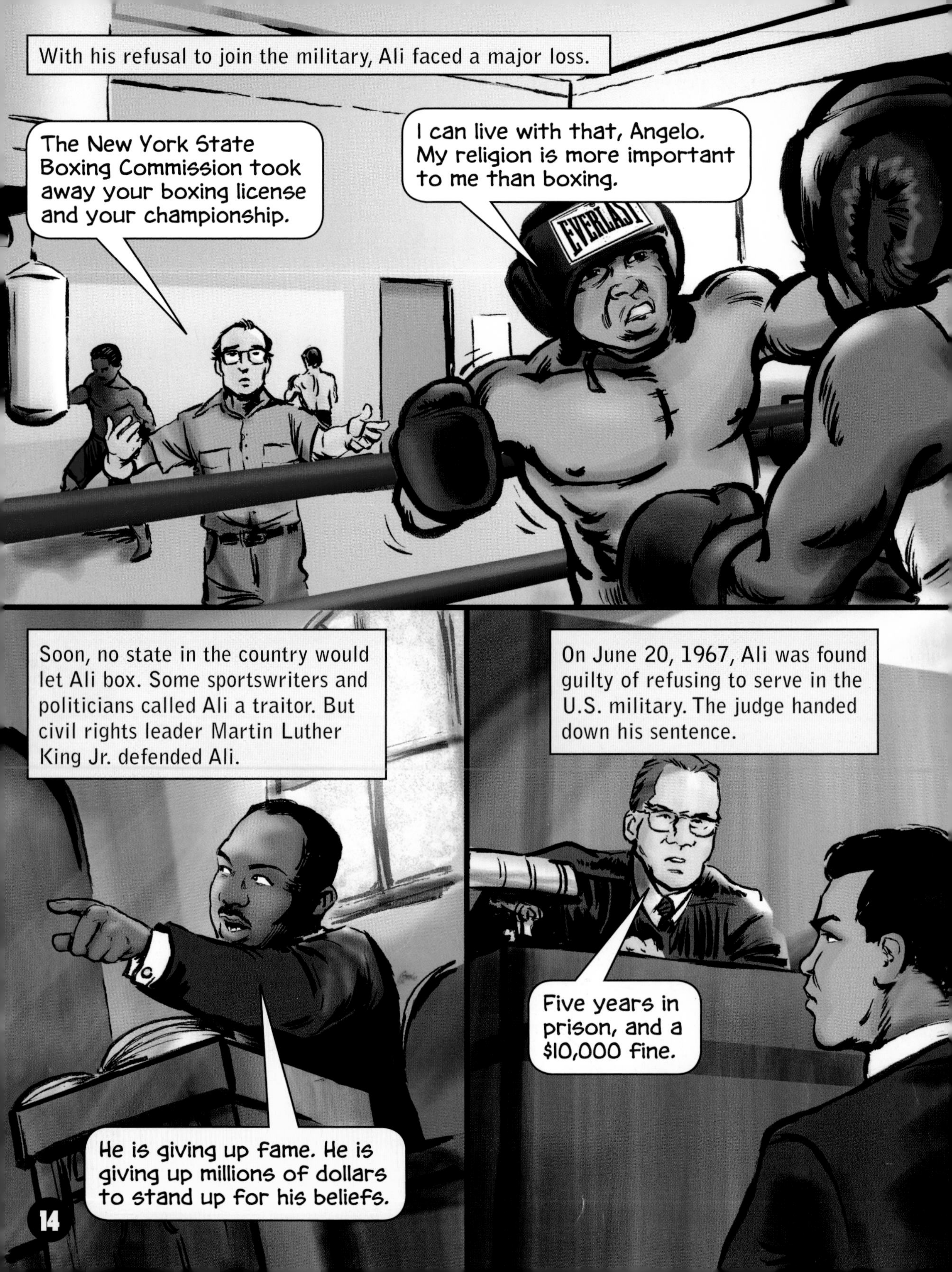
With his refusal to join the military, Ali faced a major loss.
The New York State Boxing Commission took away your boxing license and your championship.
I can live with that, Angelo. My religion is more important to me than boxing.
EVERLAST
Soon, no state in the country would let Ali box. Some sportswriters and politicians called Ali a traitor. But civil rights leader Martin Luther King Jr. defended Ali.
He is giving up fame. He is giving up millions of dollars to stand up for his beliefs.
On June 20, 1967, Ali was found guilty of refusing to serve in the U.S. military. The judge handed down his sentence.
Five years in prison, and a $10,000 fine.

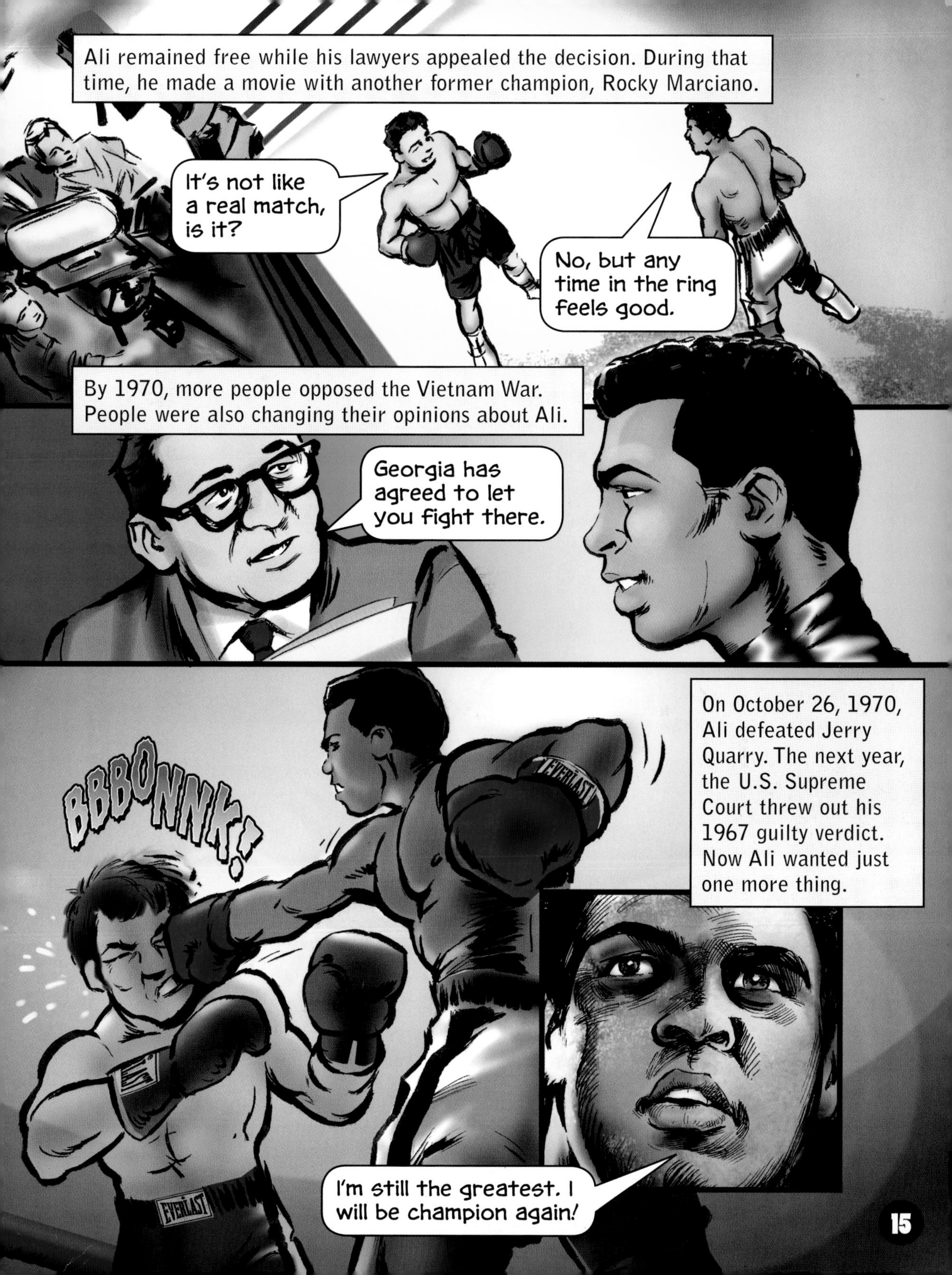

Ali remained free while his lawyers appealed the decision. During that time, he made a movie with another former champion, Rocky Marciano.
It's not like a real match, is it?
No, but any time in the ring feels good.
By 1970, more people opposed the Vietnam War. People were also changing their opinions about Ali.
Georgia has agreed to let you fight there.
BBBONNK!
On October 26, 1970, Ali defeated Jerry Quarry. The next year, the U.S. Supreme Court threw out his 1967 guilty verdict. Now Ali wanted just one more thing.
EVERLAST
I'm still the greatest. I will be champion again!

CHAPTER 3

FROM BOTTOM TO TOP

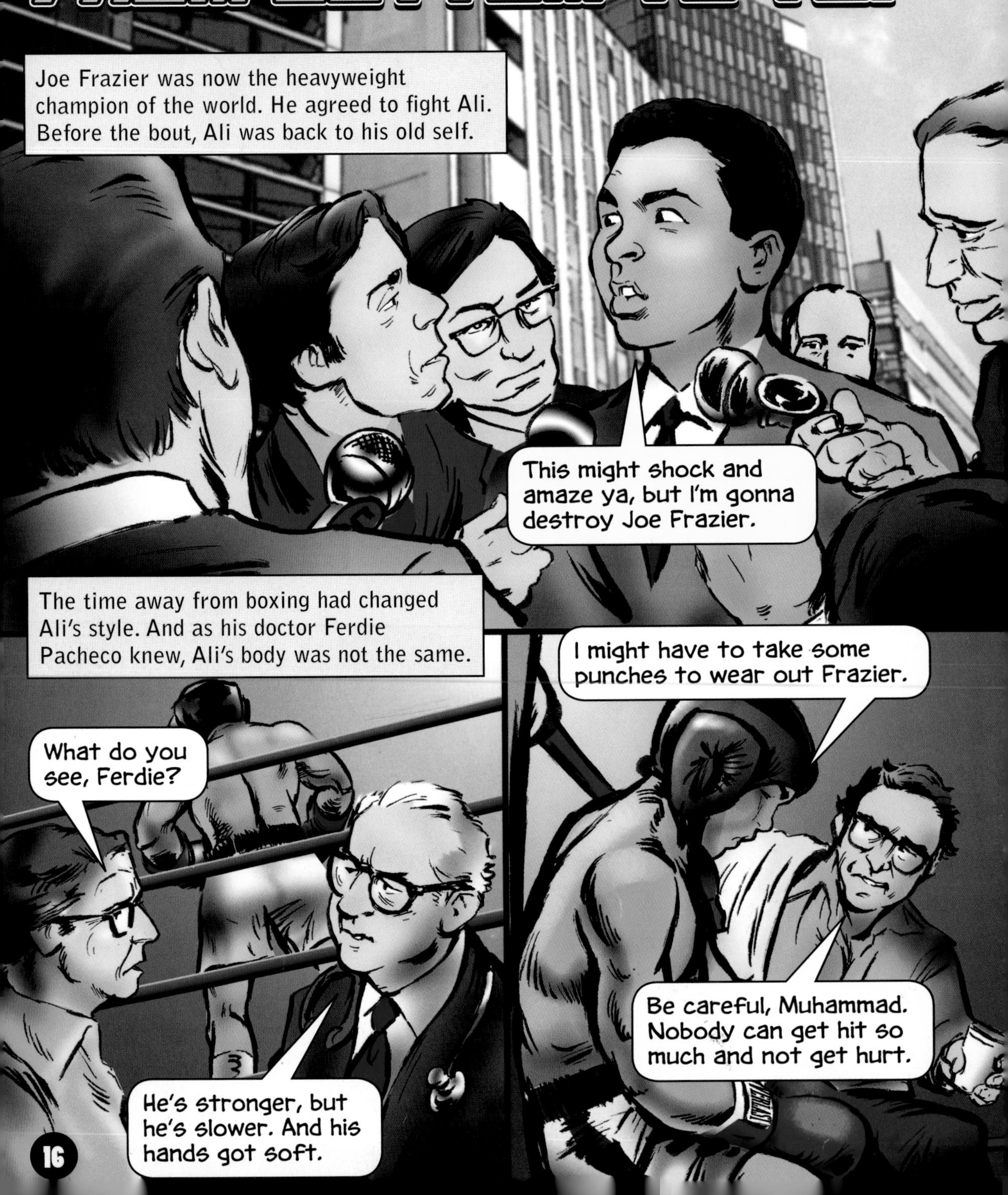

Joe Frazier was now the heavyweight champion of the world. He agreed to fight Ali. Before the bout, Ali was back to his old self.
This might shock and amaze ya, but I'm gonna destroy Joe Frazier.
The time away from boxing had changed Ali's style. And as his doctor Ferdie Pacheco knew, Ali's body was not the same.
What do you see, Ferdie?
He's stronger, but he's slower. And his hands got soft.
I might have to take some punches to wear out Frazier.
Be careful, Muhammad. Nobody can get hit so much and not get hurt.

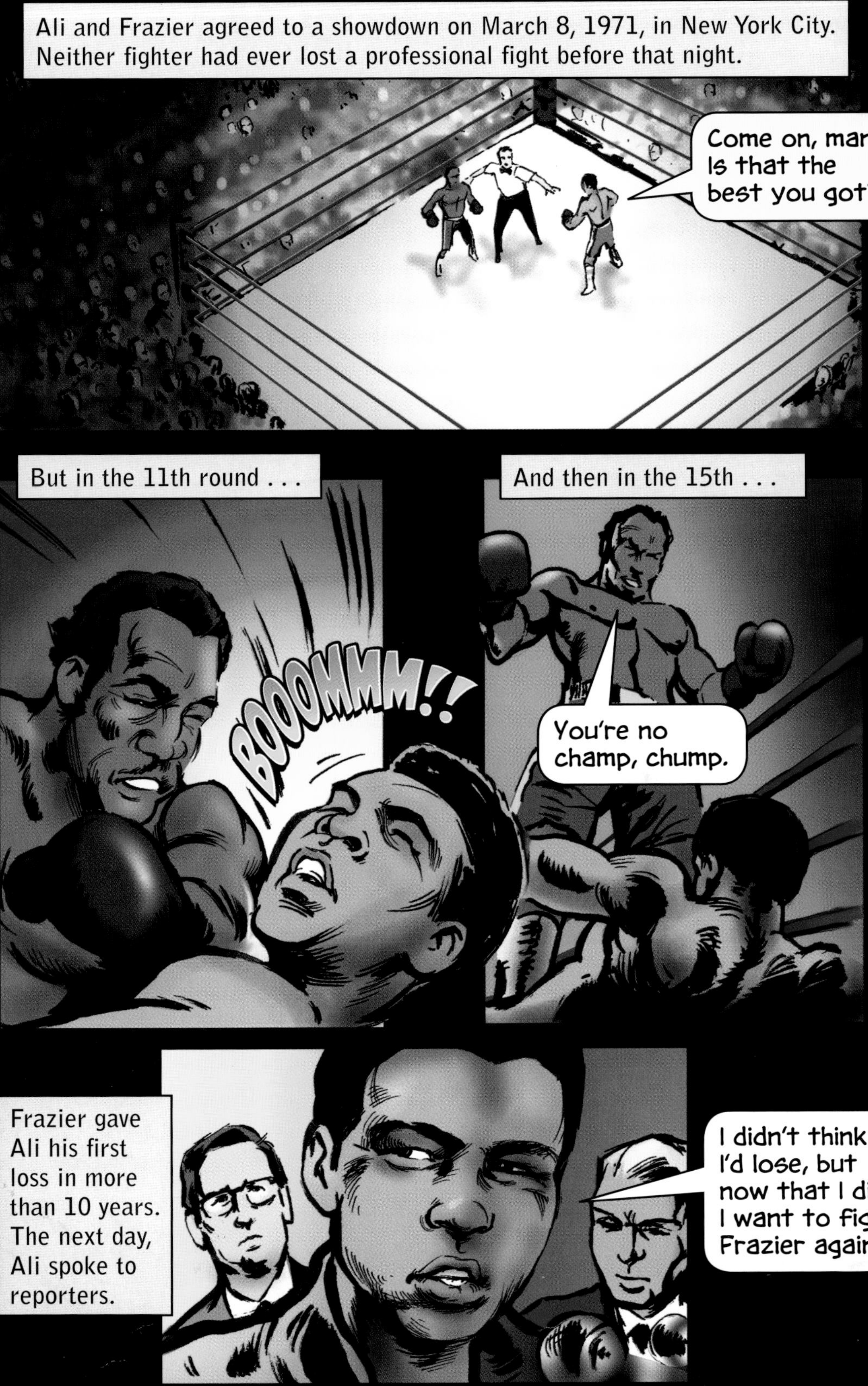
Ali and Frazier agreed to a showdown on March 8, 1971, in New York City. Neither fighter had ever lost a professional fight before that night.
Come on, man. Is that the best you got?
But in the 11th round . . .
BOOOMMM!!
And then in the 15th . . .
You're no champ, chump.
Frazier gave Ali his first loss in more than 10 years. The next day, Ali spoke to reporters.
I didn't think I'd lose, but now that I did, I want to fight Frazier again.

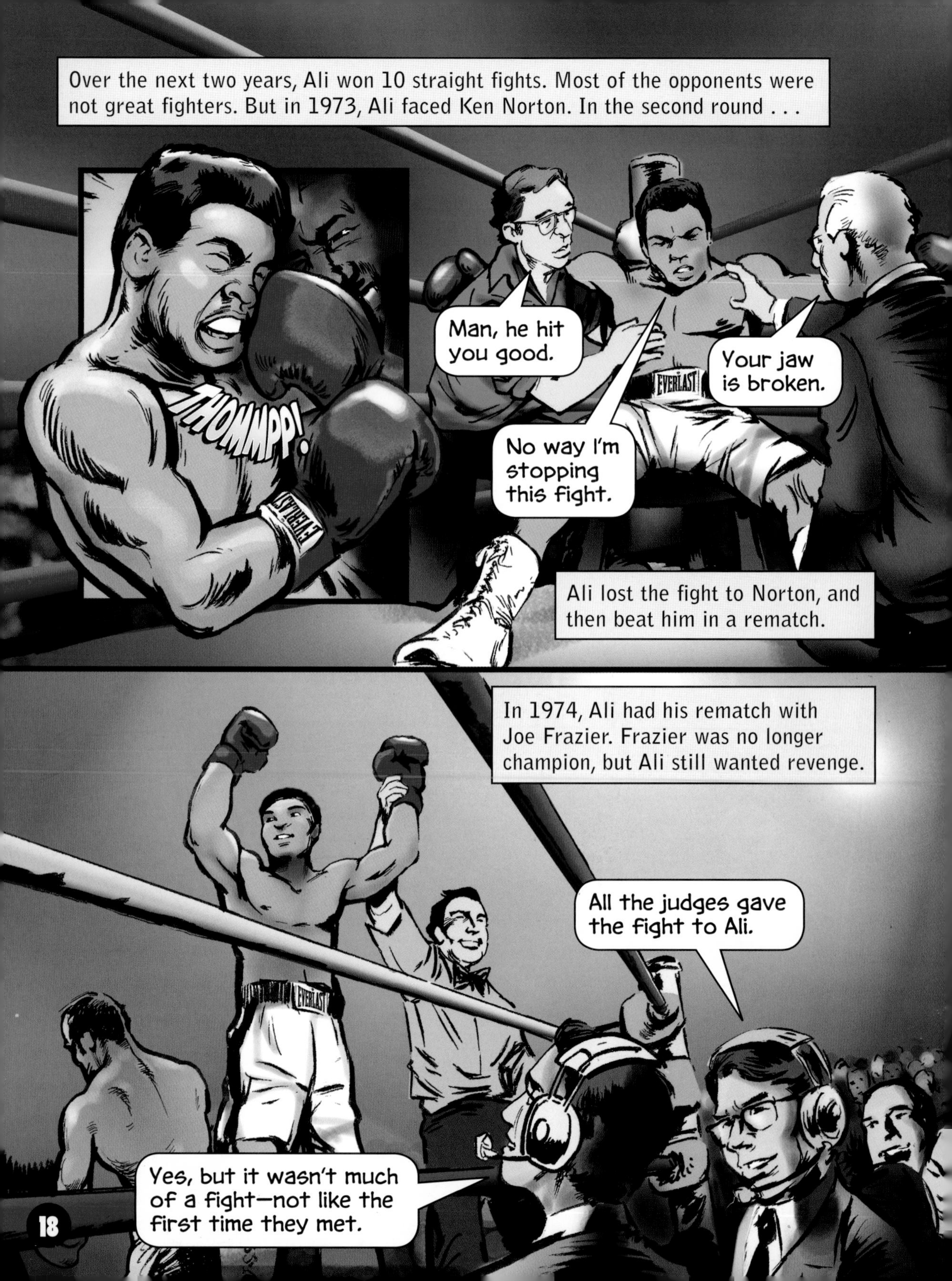
Over the next two years, Ali won 10 straight fights. Most of the opponents were not great fighters. But in 1973, Ali faced Ken Norton. In the second round . . .
THOMMPP!
EVERLAST
Man, he hit you good.
No way I'm stopping this fight.
Your jaw is broken.
EVERLAST
Ali lost the fight to Norton, and then beat him in a rematch.
In 1974, Ali had his rematch with Joe Frazier. Frazier was no longer champion, but Ali still wanted revenge.
EVERLAST
All the judges gave the fight to Ali.
Yes, but it wasn't much of a fight—not like the first time they met.

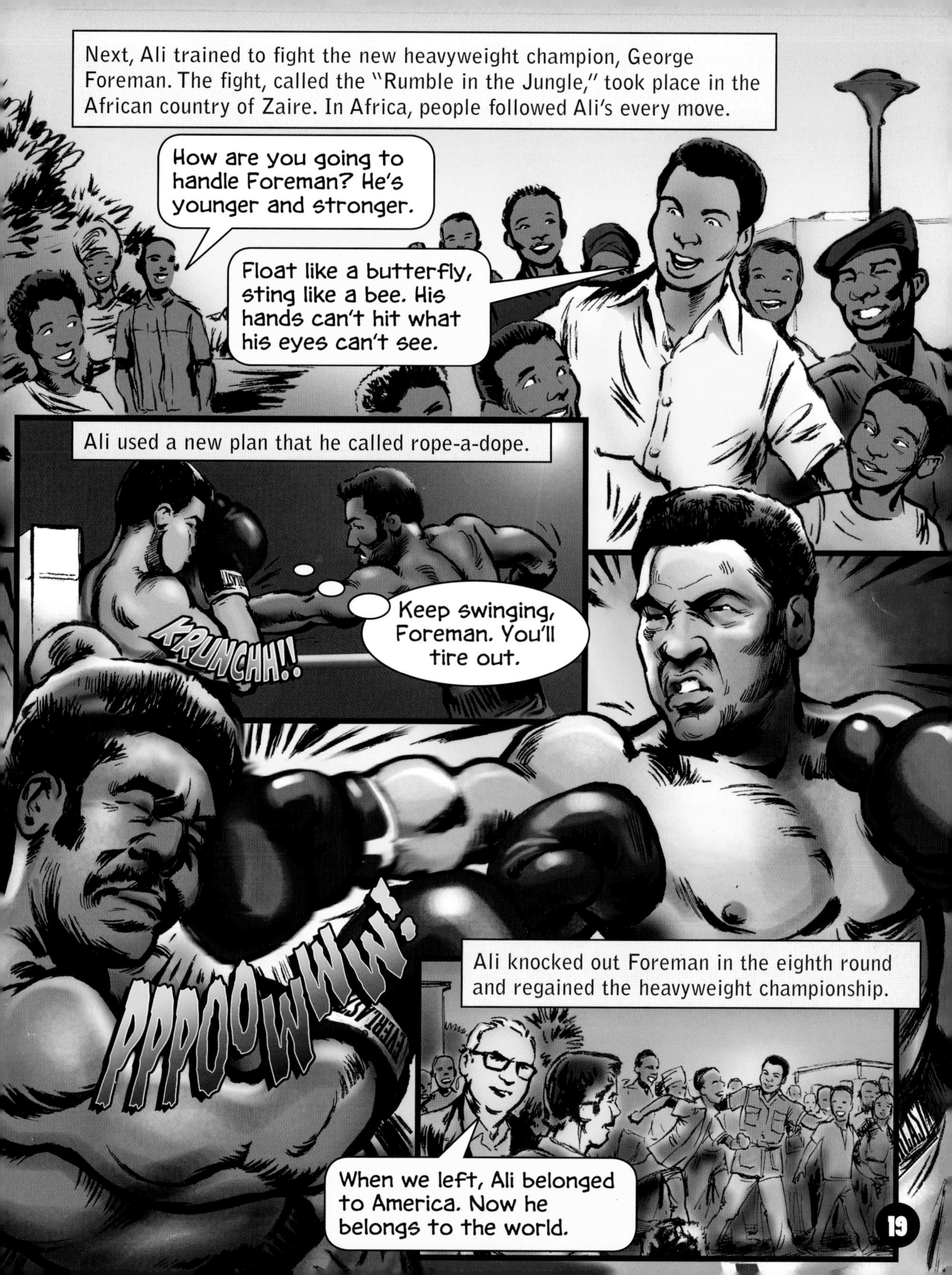
Next, Ali trained to fight the new heavyweight champion, George Foreman. The fight, called the "Rumble in the Jungle," took place in the African country of Zaire. In Africa, people followed Ali's every move.
How are you going to handle Foreman? He's younger and stronger.
Float like a butterfly, sting like a bee. His hands can't hit what his eyes can't see.
Ali used a new plan that he called rope-a-dope.
KRUNCHH!!
Keep swinging, Foreman. You'll tire out.
PPPOOWWW!
Ali knocked out Foreman in the eighth round and regained the heavyweight championship.
When we left, Ali belonged to America. Now he belongs to the world.

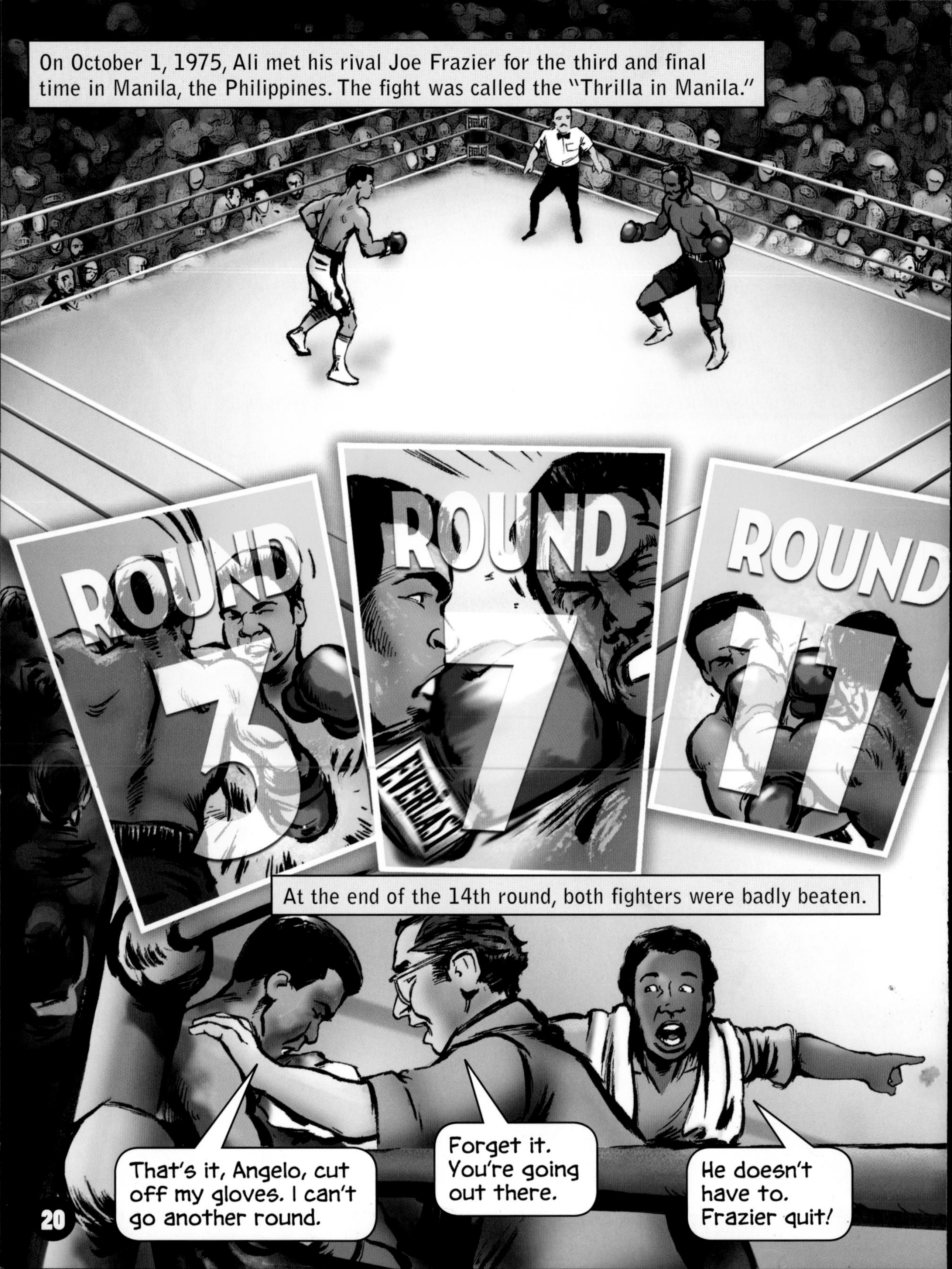
On October 1, 1975, Ali met his rival Joe Frazier for the third and final time in Manila, the Philippines. The fight was called the "Thrilla in Manila."
EVERLAST
ROUND 3
ROUND 7
EVERLAST
ROUND 11
At the end of the 14th round, both fighters were badly beaten.
That's it, Angelo, cut off my gloves. I can't go another round.
Forget it. You're going out there.
He doesn't have to. Frazier quit!

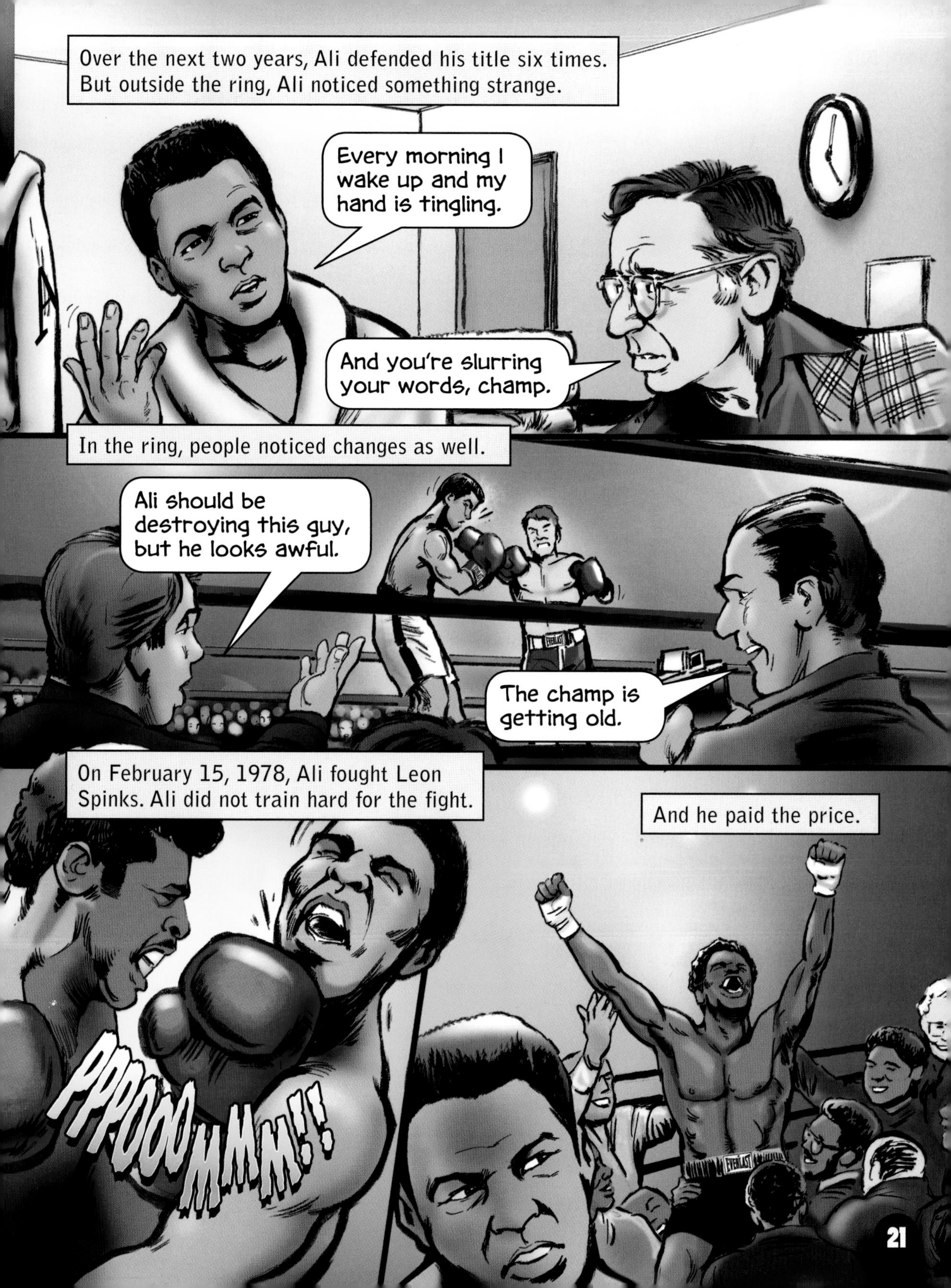
Over the next two years, Ali defended his title six times. But outside the ring, Ali noticed something strange.
Every morning I wake up and my hand is tingling.
And you're slurring your words, champ.
In the ring, people noticed changes as well.
Ali should be destroying this guy, but he looks awful.
The champ is getting old.
On February 15, 1978, Ali fought Leon Spinks. Ali did not train hard for the fight.
PPPOOOMMM!!
And he paid the price.

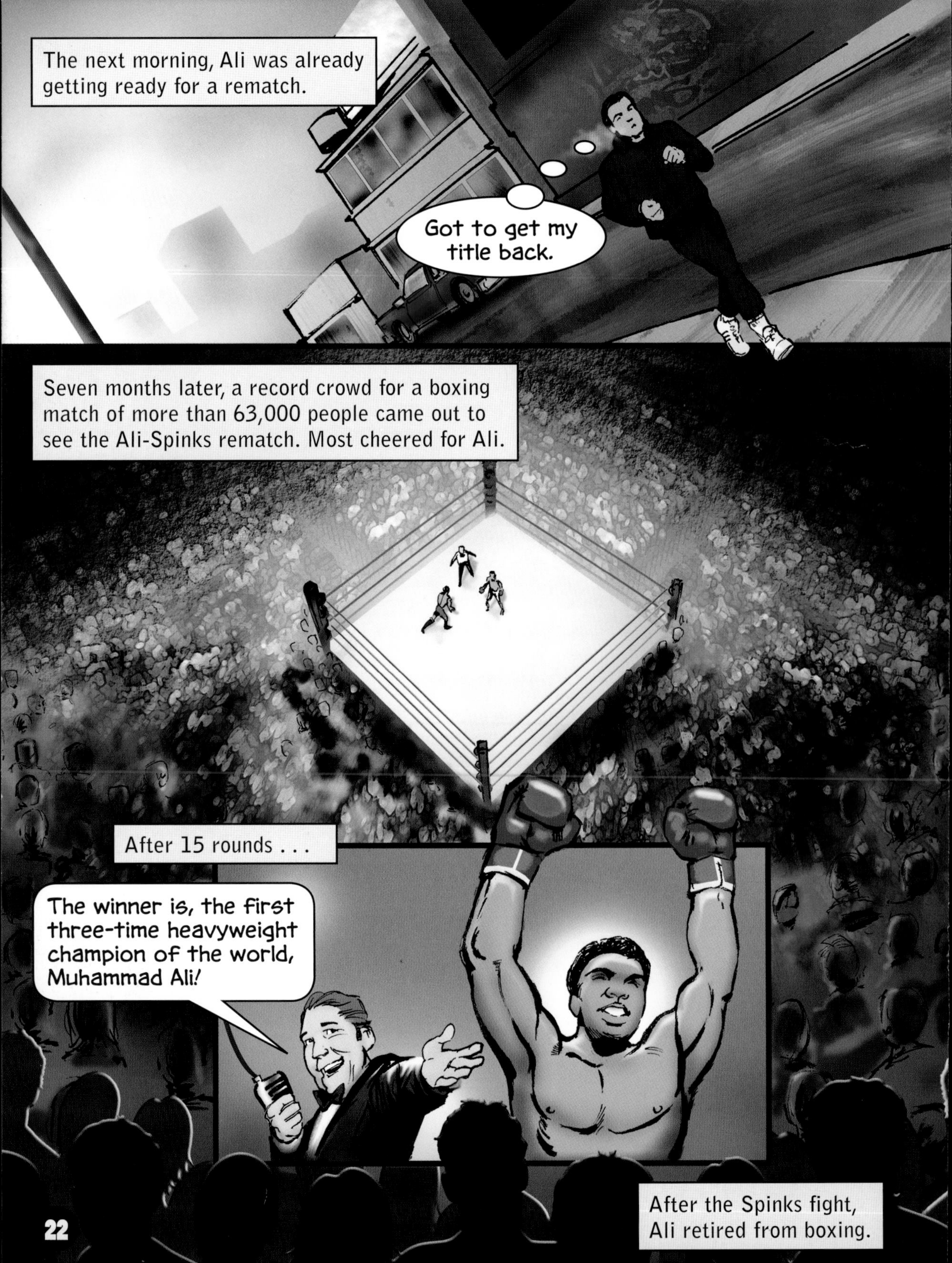

The next morning, Ali was already getting ready for a rematch.
Got to get my title back.
Seven months later, a record crowd for a boxing match of more than 63,000 people came out to see the Ali-Spinks rematch. Most cheered for Ali.
After 15 rounds . . .
The winner is, the first three-time heavyweight champion of the world, Muhammad Ali!
After the Spinks fight, Ali retired from boxing.

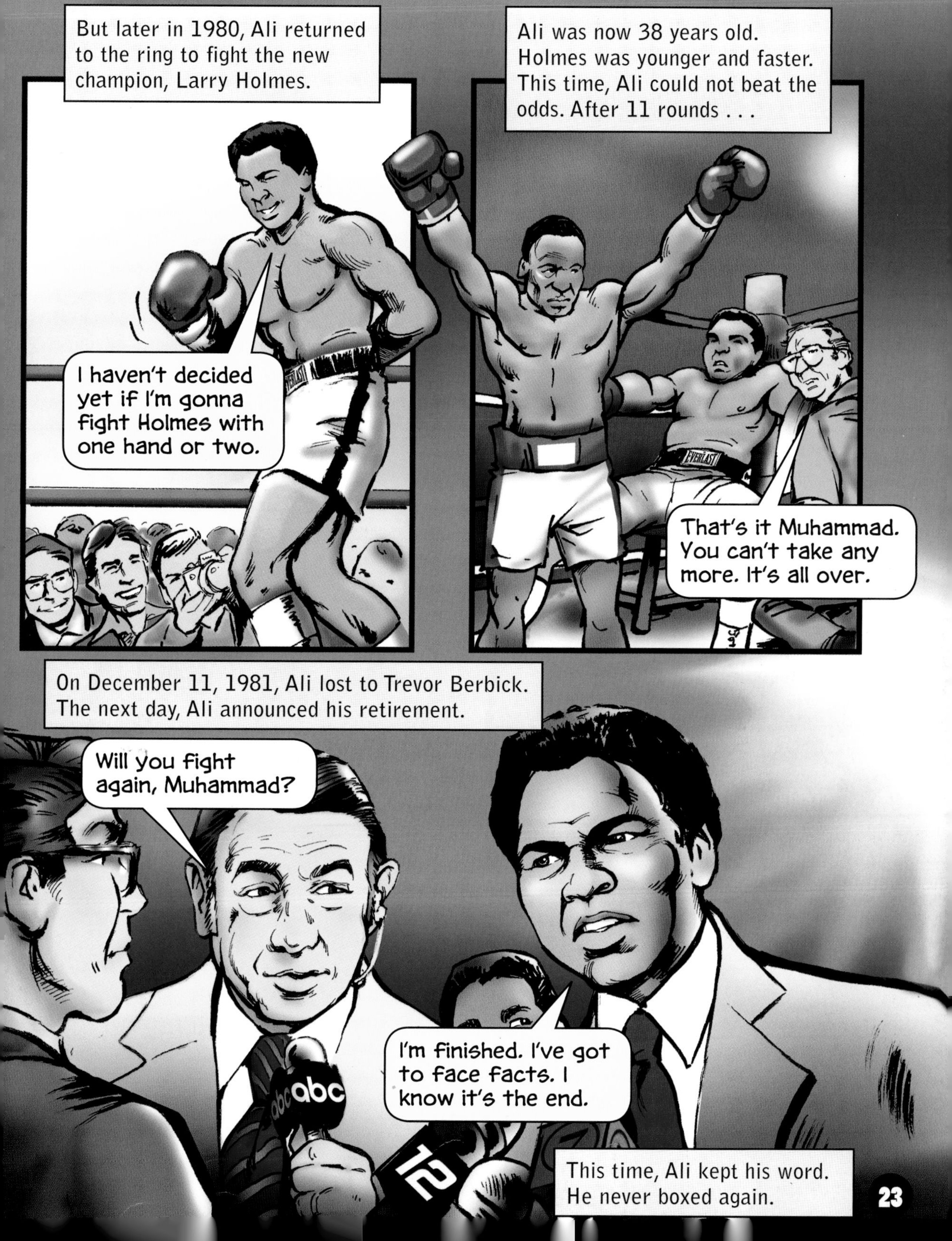

But later in 1980, Ali returned to the ring to fight the new champion, Larry Holmes.
I haven't decided yet if I'm gonna fight Holmes with one hand or two.
Ali was now 38 years old. Holmes was younger and faster. This time, Ali could not beat the odds. After 11 rounds . . .
That's it Muhammad. You can't take any more. It's all over.
On December 11, 1981, Ali lost to Trevor Berbick. The next day, Ali announced his retirement.
Will you fight again, Muhammad?
I'm finished. I've got to face facts. I know it's the end.
This time, Ali kept his word. He never boxed again.

CHAPTER 4

THE GREATEST OF ALL TIME

After his retirement, Ali remained a popular sports hero, and he helped raise money for charities. But he still faced several tough battles.

I still can't talk right. And my hand shakes.

You have Parkinson's syndrome. There's medicine that will help you feel better, but there is no cure.

Did boxing cause this disease?

Parkinson's can strike anyone.

Money also became a problem for Ali.

You made millions of dollars, but where did they all go?

When people needed money, I gave it to them.

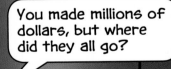

Well, now there's not much left for you.

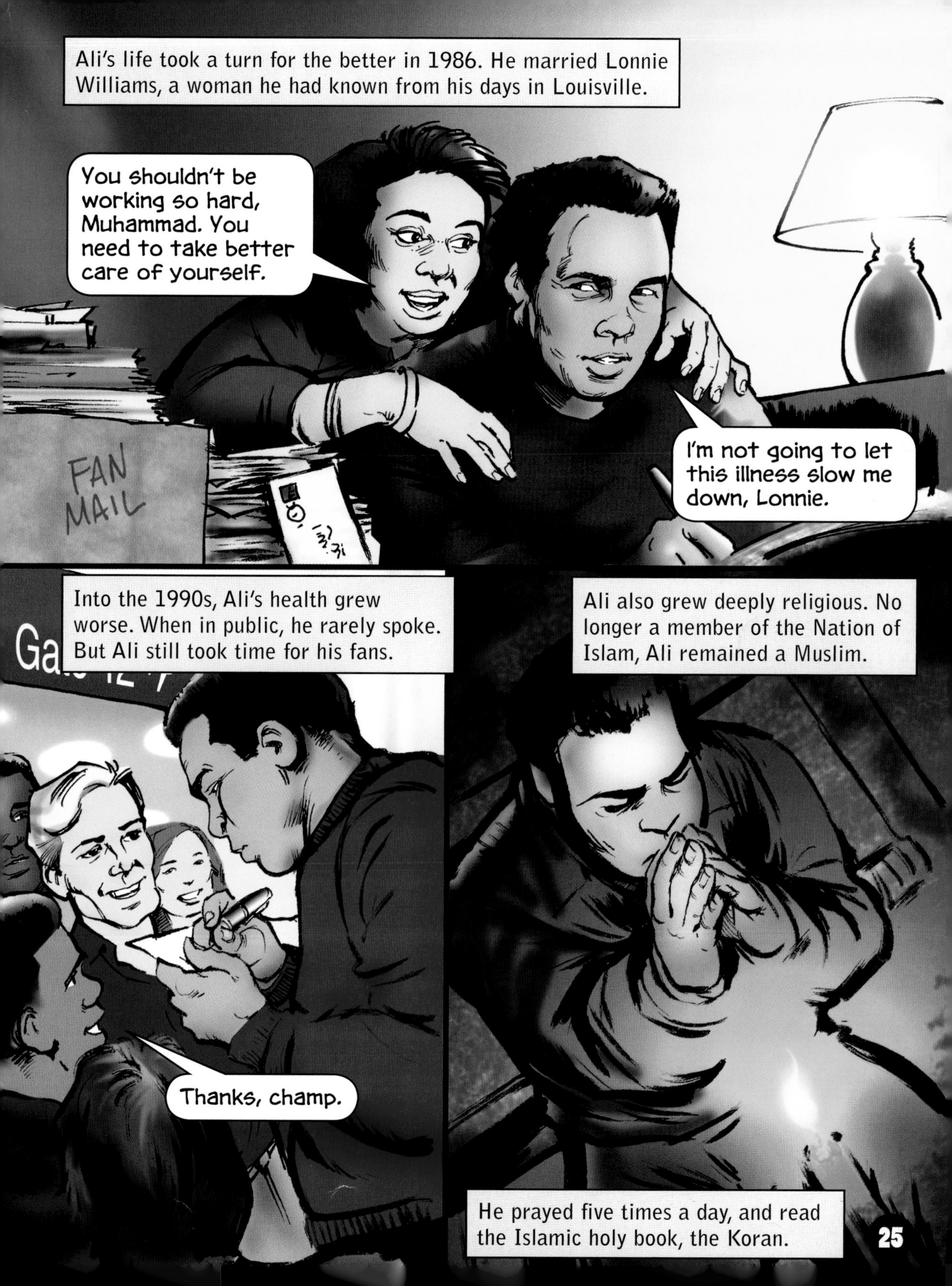
Ali's life took a turn for the better in 1986. He married Lonnie Williams, a woman he had known from his days in Louisville.
You shouldn't be working so hard, Muhammad. You need to take better care of yourself.
FAN MAIL
I'm not going to let this illness slow me down, Lonnie.
Into the 1990s, Ali's health grew worse. When in public, he rarely spoke. But Ali still took time for his fans.
Thanks, champ.
Ali also grew deeply religious. No longer a member of the Nation of Islam, Ali remained a Muslim.
He prayed five times a day, and read the Islamic holy book, the Koran.

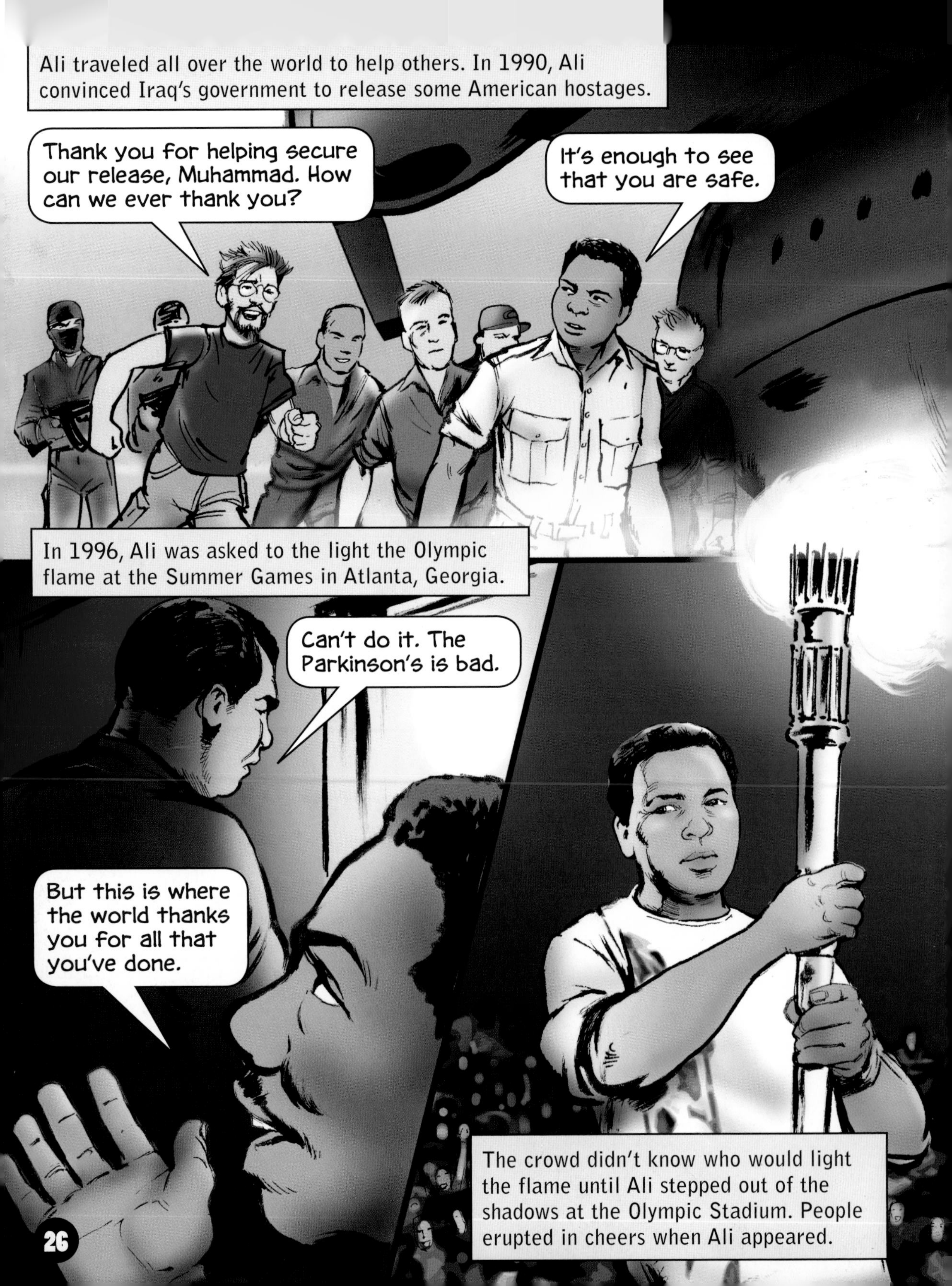
Ali traveled all over the world to help others. In 1990, Ali convinced Iraq's government to release some American hostages.
Thank you for helping secure our release, Muhammad. How can we ever thank you?
It's enough to see that you are safe.
In 1996, Ali was asked to the light the Olympic flame at the Summer Games in Atlanta, Georgia.
Can't do it. The Parkinson's is bad.
But this is where the world thanks you for all that you've done.
The crowd didn't know who would light the flame until Ali stepped out of the shadows at the Olympic Stadium. People erupted in cheers when Ali appeared.

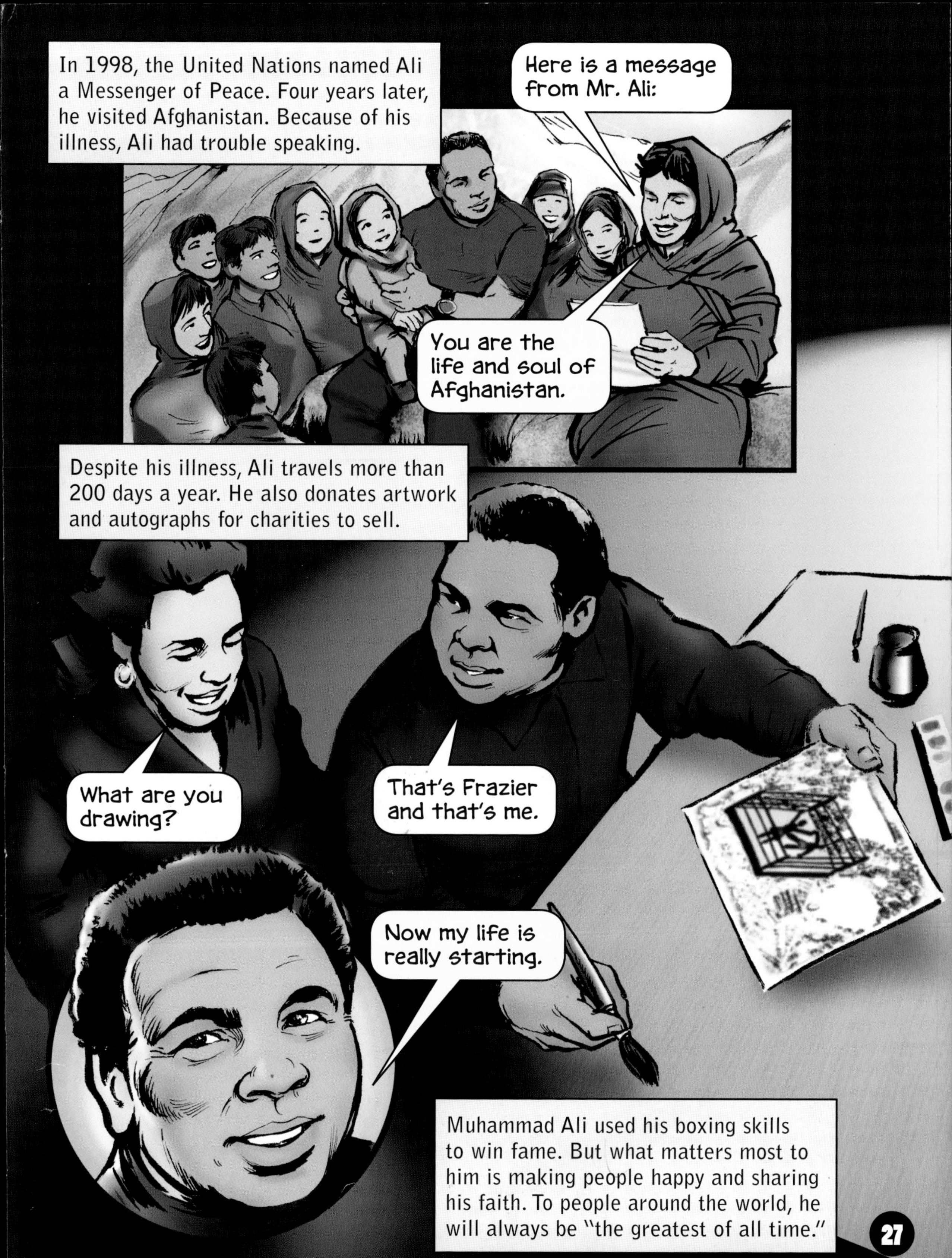
In 1998, the United Nations named Ali a Messenger of Peace. Four years later, he visited Afghanistan. Because of his illness, Ali had trouble speaking.
Here is a message from Mr. Ali:
You are the life and soul of Afghanistan.
Despite his illness, Ali travels more than 200 days a year. He also donates artwork and autographs for charities to sell.
What are you drawing?
That's Frazier and that's me.
Now my life is really starting.
Muhammad Ali used his boxing skills to win fame. But what matters most to him is making people happy and sharing his faith. To people around the world, he will always be "the greatest of all time."

MORE ABOUT
MUHAMMAD ALI

Muhammad Ali was born Cassius Clay January 17, 1942. A man named Muhammad founded the Islamic religion in AD 622. The name Muhammad means "one worthy of praise." Ali was the name of a Muslim leader. That name means "the most high."

Along with rope-a-dope, Ali invented a move called the "Ali Shuffle." He moved his feet quickly back and forth to try to confuse his opponent.

Ali ended his professional boxing career with a record of 56 wins and five losses. He won 37 of his fights by knocking out is opponent.

Ali has nine children. His daughter Laila is also a professional boxer.

Professional boxing has 17 different weight divisions. The lightest division is for boxers under 105 pounds (48 kilograms). The heavyweight division is for boxers who weigh more than 190 pounds (86 kilograms).

Ali enjoys performing magic tricks, but when he is done he always explains how the tricks work. Muslims believe they should never try to trick or deceive others.

Today doctors believe that Ali has Parkinson's disease rather than Parkinson's syndrome. The disease cannot be cured. Medicine can help control the shaking of the body that occurs with the disease.

 A book about Ali called *GOAT* (Greatest of All Time) was released in 2003. Just 10,000 copies were printed. Each book weighs 75 pounds (34 kilograms) and is signed by Ali. Some copies of the book have sold for $12,500.

 In 2005, the Muhammad Ali Center opened in Louisville, Kentucky. The center offers educational programs meant to promote respect and hope.

 In 2005, President George W. Bush gave Ali the Presidential Medal of Freedom. This medal is the highest honor given to American civilians.

GLOSSARY

amateur (AM-uh-chur)—someone who participates in a sport without being paid

draft (DRAFT)—to select young men to serve in the military

integration (in-tuh-GRAY-shuhn)—the practice of including people of all races in schools and other public places

Islam (ISS-luhm)—the religion of Muslims, based on the teachings of the prophet Muhammad

mentor (MEN-tur)—a wise and faithful adviser or teacher

prejudice (PREJ-uh-diss)—hatred or unfair treatment of others based on their race or religion

Vietcong (VEE-et-kohng)—Vietnam communists who fought against the United States during the Vietnam War (1954-1975)

INTERNET SITES

FactHound offers a safe, fun way to find Internet sites related to this book. All of the sites on FactHound have been researched by our staff.

Here's how:
1. Visit *www.facthound.com*
2. Choose your grade level.
3. Type in this book ID **1429601531** for age-appropriate sites. You may also browse subjects by clicking on letters, or by clicking on pictures and words.
4. Click on the **Fetch It** button.

FactHound will fetch the best sites for you!

READ MORE

Ali, Maryum. *I Shook Up the World: The Incredible Life of Muhammad Ali.* Milwaukee: Gareth Stevens, 2004.

Ali, Rasheda. *I'll Hold Your Hand So You Won't Fall: A Child's Guide to Parkinson's Disease.* West Palm Beach, Fla.: Merit Publishing International, 2005.

Feinstein, Stephen. *Muhammad Ali.* African-American Heroes. Berkeley Heights, N.J.: Enslow: 2007.

Self, David. *Islam.* Religions of the World. Milwaukee: World Almanac Library, 2006.

Wood, Don. *A World-Class Boxer.* The Making of a Champion. Chicago: Heinemann, 2005.

BIBLIOGRAPHY

Ali, Muhammad. *The Soul of a Butterfly: Reflections on Life's Journey.* New York: Simon & Schuster, 2004.

Early, Gerald, editor. *The Muhammad Ali Reader.* Hopewell, N.J.: Ecco Press, 1998.

Hauser, Thomas. *Muhammad Ali: His Life and Times.* New York: Simon & Schuster, 1991.

Remnick, David. *King of the World: Muhammad Ali and the Rise of an American Hero.* New York: Random House, 1998.

INDEX